Self-Publishing

Self-Publishing

Detailed step by step guide to self-publish your books

MAXIMO KOVAK

SELF-PUBLISHING
Detailed step by step guide to self-publish your books

Published by Maximo Kovak
www.maximokovak.com

Copyright © 2013 Maximo Kovak

All rights reserved. No part of this book may be used or reproduced in any manner whatsoever including Internet usage, without written permission of the author.

Book design by Maureen Cutajar
www.gopublished.com

English edition Paperback ISBN 978-0-9575953-3-0
English edition Ebook ISBN 978-0-9575953-4-7

Spanish edition Paperback ISBN 978-0-9575953-5-4
Spanish edition Ebook ISBN 978-0-9575953-6-1

CONTENTS

INTRODUCTION
Are you sure you want to self-publish? 1
Where can I self-publish my book? 2
My number 1 advice for new authors trying to self-publish is: 4
Email support by Maximo Kovak 5

CHAPTER ONE
Things To Do and Consider Before Self-Publishing 7
Finish your book 7
The length. Too short or too long? 8
Your book's title 11
The synopsis 12
The cover design 12
Copy editing your book 14
Pen name / or your real name? Copyright. 16
Applying for tax exemption in the USA 17
Getting your ISBN numbers 27
Getting your barcode for your print edition 31
Formatting your book 34
Creating your marketing plan. 36
Before publishing checklist 38

CHAPTER TWO
Publishing Your Book 39

CHAPTER THREE
Submitting Your Book 41

CHAPTER FOUR 43
Marketing Your Book 43
- Choosing the right genre categories: 43
- Creating your own website 45
- Targeting audience 52
- Selling your book in independent bookshops 54
- Media and advertising 57
- Book reviews and book contests 59
- Marketing stationery 64
- Maximising social networks 65
- Your office: being organised 67
- Distribute sample chapters 68
- Promote your book's URL in your email signature 69
- Don't stop promoting one book to start writing another ... 69
- Rock your book's trailer. 69
- Free sites for e-book promotion 70
- Blogging 72

CONCLUSION 77

INTRODUCTION

This book provides useful information and advice for authors and writers who decide to go down the self-publishing route. It will provide you with a step by step organised guide to self-publishing your book and will help you to avoid mistakes, saving money and time.

This guide does not include a magic wand or every single answer you might need; however, you will find here many practical answers that are not provided in other guides and – most importantly – tips to help you get organised during the decision-making process.

Are you sure you want to self-publish?

"Are you crazy? Self-publishing is a waste of time; it is for losers and authors who failed to find agents or publishers!"

This is what I had to hear when I tried self-publishing, but now I have my books in the hands of many readers, thanks to my persistence.

Self-publishing is not a bed of roses and involves a lot of hours of work and research, being extremely organised, focused and patient. If you don't have these qualities, perhaps this is not the right path for you.

On top of all that, you will need a budget. Self-publishing does not come for free.

You will have to do all the work publishers do for authors yourself and you will have to learn many new things on the go to avoid mistakes and make your adventure a success. But the benefits of all that hard work are:

- You will have more control over your book.
- You will get the chance to make more profit from your book.
- You will learn many new things about publishing.

The work does not finish when you write the book, after that there is a long process over many months of working hard, getting your book ready according to the publishing standards required, hiring and choosing professionals to help you in achieving that, getting advice, reading and researching, and once your book is online and ready for the readers, you will have to apply your own marketing strategy to increase sales. Hard work! But not impossible.

During your first attempt at self-publishing, you will realise that there are many people and companies trying to get your money and rip you off. They are the publishing sharks, be aware of them and never pay for any service you could do yourself or find much cheaper elsewhere by doing some research.

Where can I self-publish my book?

The self-publishing market is buzzing. Many authors are now taking the self-publishing route rather than approaching publishers or agents. Several companies are already offering a very professional service for self-publishing; the bigger ones are:

Bubok.com – Very easy to use, language friendly with website menus in English, Spanish, Portuguese and French. You can publish your book as an e-book or a paperback with them. The submission of books is free and they have good customer service and a phone support line.

CreateSpace.com – This company is linked to Amazon and gives you the chance to publish your e-book on Kindle and also as a print on demand (POD) paperback. No publishing fee is required, but they charge a percentage per book sold. No phone support line.

Smashwords.com – This company will publish your e-book edition only, but they distribute to the most important companies: Apple iBookstore, Barnes & Noble, Sony Reader Store, Kobo, the Diesel E-book Store, Baker & Taylor's Blio and Axis360, etc. No publishing fee is required, but they charge a percentage per book sold. No phone support line.

Lulu.com – Easy to use self-publishing service for paperback and hardcover books. A fee might apply depending on the options you select. They also offer e-book format options. They have a phone support line.

Other pages where you can also self-publish your eBooks and printed editions are:

- Kindle (digital) www.amazon.es/kindle
- liibook (www.liibook.com)
- Blurb (printed) www.blurb.co.uk/?redirect=true
- XinXii (printed) http://www.xinxii.com/en
- Scribd.com (digital) www.scribd.com
- FastPencil Inc www.fastpencil.com
- Punto Didot (printed) www.puntodidot.com/ (Books in Spanish)
- Upabook (digital) www.upabook.com

Self-Publishing

My number 1 advice for new authors trying to self-publish is:

Research, research, more research. During the process you will have many questions to ask and decisions to make. When you are not sure, do not get stacked:

1. Go to Google and search on your question there, you will be surprised how many useful blogs and answers you will find.
2. Visit the blogs for users at CreateSpace and Smashwords, where authors help each other by sharing knowledge and answering questions. You get sometimes answers on the same day, but a response might take several days, so be patient.
3. Read specialised books related to the subject – like this one – where you will find practical solutions and advice. Before you buy them, read the reviews and try to get an idea of the contents. Many books include a preview online.

I bought four books related to self-publishing and I learnt many tricks, but some of them were very general and I did not get the answers to the small issues and questions that came up along the way. I realised that information was essential for me to succeed in the process. I needed a guide explaining to me step by step how to self-publish, starting from the very beginning, but I could not find it. I ended up collecting all the info from different places and sources, which was very time-consuming and tiring.

That is the reason I decided to write this book: to help new authors not only by describing the general aspects of self-publishing, but also by providing answers to the small challenges and questions I faced myself.

Introduction

Email support by Maximo Kovak

I know how difficult the process is and how frustrating it is to wait for answers, so I have decided to offer my readers the chance to contact me directly to ask any questions related to self-publishing that they might have. Bear in mind that I receive dozens of questions per week and so I might not be able to answer immediately, but you will get a personal answer from me, for sure.

This service is exclusively available for readers of this book. You will have to supply the **email support code** provided at the end of the book as the headline on your email when you contact me, for me to answer any related questions. Reading the book first will help to avoid unnecessary questions that have been already answered.

CHAPTER ONE

Things To Do and Consider Before Self-Publishing

Finish your book

I assume you have already finished your book or you are in the process of finishing it.

You cannot self-publish without having a manuscript ready.

Have you finished your book yet? Are you ready to publish it?

Hold on a moment. I would advise you to put your manuscript in the drawer for one or two weeks and take a break. You think that I am crazy, don't you?

Most new authors want everything to be done fast, they want to see the end of the process and to be able to relax. Well, I am afraid it is not that easy.

Slow down a bit and remember the final goal is for people to read your book. You need to be happy with what you wrote and so you should review your book at least once or twice before settling on the final version.

In addition, when you send your manuscript for editing you want to make sure that it is the final version and all the additions or cuts needed have already been amended. To send a manuscript that has not been reviewed properly will cost you extra money, as the editor will have double the work to do. The reason for putting the book in a drawer and taking a mini break is to give your mind a rest from what you wrote so when you come back and read it again you can be more objective. This will help you to find flaws or mistakes, perhaps even identify new things that you can add, or sections that don't work and can be removed. Basically, this is the chance to polish your book and make it read exactly as you want it to.

If you have good contacts or friends who are journalists or writers, do not hesitate to ask them to read some of your chapters, or even the whole book, for review. They might give you some tips or ideas to improve your book.

During the process of writing your book you should also think about the market you are targeting. For example, when I wrote my book "First Floor Room 16", I knew the main market for that book was the gay and lesbian community, as the theme was related to them; however, I also wanted to appeal to middle-aged ladies and straight males curious about the subject. While writing the book, I made sure that the scenes and situations had enough spice to entertain the LGBT community, but not too much to put off the other targets.

Remember, you won't have real publishers reviewing your book before launch so to guarantee that you are selling material that won't embarrass you and is of good quality, you need to review you book before even it is copy edited. Low quality books don't sell.

The length. Too short or too long?

When I wrote my first book, I was not aware that the length of my book would affect many factors during publishing, such as:

The cost of copy editing and formatting. It does not cost the same to edit a book of 120 pages and a book of 400 pages, and the same goes for formatting. The longer your book, the higher the cost. The prices shown below are just examples and might vary depending on the company or professional you have selected to do that job, but they will give an idea of how length affects cost.

	100-250 Pages			250-450 Pages		
Copy-editing	£200-£300	$300-$450	€230-€345	£500-£700	$748-$1,050	€572-€800
E-book formatting	£30	$45	€35	£100	$150	€115
Paperback formatting	£55	$80	€63	£150	$225	€172

The cost of print on demand publishing. Many authors wish to have their books published not only as e-books, but also in paperback. Formatting for paperback is different to formatting for e-books; therefore you will have an extra cost when preparing your book for paperback publishing. On the top of that, the length of your book will influence the printing cost and therefore the price you can sell it for.

I would suggest trying the royalty calculator on the CreateSpace website, where you can clearly see how the number of pages affects the selling price and the royalty you will get. Use the link below and select the "Royalties" tab, then choose the standard trim size 5.5 inches x 8.5 inches in the calculator. https://www.CreateSpace.com/Products/Book

Have you already played with the royalty calculator? Well, I guess you have seen already how the length of your book (number of pages) directly affects the selling price. The higher the price, the less competitive your book will appear against other titles which sell for a lower price. On the other hand, if you price your book very low then you won't make much in royalties, therefore little or no profit from your paperback edition. It is like a trap, isn't it? Well, the solution is not that complicated. Writing books that are neither too long nor too short makes it easier when playing with pricing and royalties. Books with around 150-250 pages are much easier to manage than books with 400 pages, when self-publishing.

Choosing the trim size for your print edition is also connected to your book length. The two most popular standard book sizes are 6 inches x 9 inches and 5.5 inches x 8.5 inches. Longer books will benefit from the 6 inches x 9 inches page size, as it is bigger and it will reduce the page count when formatting the book. Conversely, if your book is short you will derive benefit from the extra pages gained when using 5.5 inches x 8.5 inches. It is your book; you can decide how you want it. You will need to decide what trim size you want to use for your printed edition before it is formatted and published.

How shall I price my book? That is the big question. People will tell you different things, but what do not lie are the present market and the price points that consistently sell more. And again, the length of your book will affect the pricing range you can play with. The price for e-books is much lower than for paperbacks for obvious reasons, readers know the production cost is lower, so they expect to pay less. When you try to publish your e-book via CreateSpace, Lulu or Smashwords, you realise that they indirectly push authors to lower their prices by having search sections called "E-books for $2.99 or less". As a new, **unknown author,** you will have to get your book pricing strategy right.

If you are just publishing your book to have the satisfaction of having friends and family enjoy your masterpiece, then the price can be as high as you wish; but if you are considering making a proper marketing strategy and selling as much as you can, then your prices should be competitive and lower. Every time I encountered a Kindle reader on a train or on the street I asked them the same question: "What is your price criteria when buying e-books?" Most of them recognised that they will never spend more than £5 / $7.50 on an e-book, and if they can get two for that price, even better. They also confessed that they follow and search through the bestsellers list to find a good book.

Here you go!!! You have to get to the bestseller list to really push your book sales, and to do that you have to price your e-book competitively. To achieve that you will have to work hard on your marketing strategy.

When you check e-book prices you will notice that non-fiction books are priced a bit higher than fiction, but again, this will depend on many factors including who the author is, the book length, and other aspects besides.

On the other hand, if you are planning to have a paperback edition, you should know the price range is very different.

I priced my first book at £2.99 for the e-book version and £4.99 for the paperback. I was so tempted to charge £8.99 for the paperback edition, but after serious thought I realised that it is better to sell more at a lower price than a few at a higher price. The right time to take decisions about your book pricing is while your book is being copy edited, as just after that stage you will have to take several steps for which the price will have to have been set.

Your book's title

Choosing the right title turned out to be more important than I expected and it also affected different areas:

- Your title will be competing with thousands of others, so it should be catchy and give an idea about the contents of the book. You can have a main title and a subtitle giving extra information, but that is your choice.
- If you choose a title that includes wording similar to other titles already published, when potential readers search for your book they might not find it as many other titles will come up first, jeopardising your chances to sell. Write down title options and search in online stores like Amazon or Apple books to check that no one else has used similar titles or words.

- If you want to use a website to promote your book using the book's title as the domain name, you should check that the domain is available before taking a final decision. If you want to use your author name as the domain name, don't waste time: check immediately whether it is available and get it before anyone else does. More about creating a website and domains later.

The synopsis

Once you've finished your book and it is being copy edited, you can start working on your synopsis. You will need two of them:

- A short one, where you condense a description of your book into about three or four sentences. This short description will be required when you register your book for publishing and it will be the first thing potential readers will see, so work hard on it.
- A longer synopsis, where you describe your book in three or four paragraphs maximum (about half a page). You will need this longer synopsis for the registration of your book, too, but you can also use it as a template for press releases and for the back cover text of your book. So be creative!!

The cover design

After the synopsis you can start working on your cover design.
You might be thinking, but I have never designed a cover before! Neither had I. You don't need to be Picasso.
If your budget is big enough, you can opt for the services provided for authors at CreateSpace and Smashwords, but I personally think that they are a total rip off. You can save a lot of money by finding

professionals yourself. If you have experience using Photoshop or Publisher software you can play around with images and fonts, getting an idea of what you want.

If you don't have a clue about design software, there are still things that you can do:

1. Think about what type of image you would like to have on your cover. You can buy online for a reasonable price stock photos that you can use for your book cover. Google "stock photos" and you will find many companies which sell high resolution images. You can search by keyword on their site and find the right photo for you. I personally use one website called colourbox.com as they guarantee the rights for book covers and publishing. The price per photo is about €10. Make sure you keep the receipt for purchase in your files as you might need to prove you hold the rights for that image at some point. It will also come in useful when you do your accounts.
2. At this point you should already know your title. Play around with the fonts and colours to get an idea about how your title could look on your book cover.

By doing that little bit of work yourself you could save a lot of money. Getting a designer to do your cover from scratch (with you not providing any images or ideas) could cost you around $200-$300; however, if you provide the images you want to use plus some ideas, you will be asking for a design collaboration and the cost could drop to as little as $70.

When you speak with the designers make sure you tell them where you are planning to publish your book, as each company has slightly different submission requirements related to format, sizes, etc. The designer will need to know the trim size, interior paper colour, and total page count of your book (to work out the size of the spine); therefore you cannot complete the cover design until your book has been copy edited and formatted for the print edition, and any necessary blank pages have been added.

There are many places where you can find cover designers but I would suggest checking peopleperhour.com and fiverr.com for low or medium budgets. Remember that in this case you are working with just one designer and whatever the result, you will have to pay him. You have to be very organised and do your research to avoid mistakes when using this option.

Is this you?

1. I would prefer to have more than one designer making proposals.
2. I am not very good at design. I prefer people to do it for me.
3. I want a great book cover and I have a generous budget for that of around $200.

If so, I would suggest you post a design request on a specialised website like 99designs.co.uk/book-cover-design. On these types of websites you can open a design request / contest explaining what you need and how much you are willing to pay. Designers will accept the challenge and create a design proposal for you before the deadline. This is the perfect way to get a good cover when you are not sure about what you want. You will get different type of design proposals and you can choose the one most suitable for your book. This is less risky than placing all your cards with just one designer, but a bit more expensive.

Copy editing your book

This is of course a personal decision but if you have completed your memoir / novel / non-fiction book and plan to upload it to Amazon or

Smashwords or one of the many other self-publishing websites, yes, you need an editor. Before you self-publish, your book needs to be as perfect as possible, and that means hiring someone to copy edit your manuscript for grammatical, spelling, punctuation, and typographical errors.

What is the difference between copy editing and formatting?

Typically, copy editing involves correcting spelling, punctuation, grammar, terminology, jargon, and semantics, and ensuring that the text adheres to the publisher's style (you) and follows the professional standards required for publishing.

A book formatter prepares your book for printing or e-book according to the guidelines of the site you will be submitting to. Formatters won't necessarily read your book or correct any grammar mistakes; they just adjust the text and style to the requirements, facilitating an easy upload of your book on the sites you have chosen and guaranteeing a more professional look for your book. Formatting for e-book is different to formatting for print so you will need to get two different formatting if you wish to publish in both formats.

The process of copy editing could take between two to four weeks, depending on the length of your book. Copy editing is the most expensive part of the process, it will cost you around $300 for a book with 100 pages.

To find editors you can:

- Google "Book editors associations", or "book editors freelance," followed by your country name.
- Also, you can search for editors on the forums and blogs at CreateSpace and Smashwords.
- Or try specialised websites where freelancers offer their services, like peopleperhour.com. Use the search box to find book editors or copy editors. I use this website often when I need to find professionals like web designers, programmers, formatters, etc. You can open a profile and post a

job advert explaining what you need and stating your budget. People will then reply to you with their proposals. The sites have tools to rate the professionals similar to the ones used on eBay so you can get an idea if they are good or not before accepting any proposal. By reading their portfolio details you can also get an overview of their experience and see whether that person is the one best suited for your job. But the handier tool is the method of payment. Once you agree a fee you don't pay the freelancer directly, but through the website. Normally payment is held by the website until the job is done and has been reviewed by you, but sometimes they may ask for a small payment in advance of around 10% or 20% of the total. I think that is reasonable. I would suggest keeping all communications during the process through the website so if you have any problems after you can prove that it was not your fault and Peopleperhour will refund your money. They provide phone customer support for all users.

Pen name / or your real name? Copyright.

I knew from the beginning that as an author I would be using a pen name rather than my real name. Some of my books include adult erotic content, so I did not want to reveal my real name. I had serious concerns about how that would affect my copyright ownership, but after a lot of research and confusion I found an easy solution that works whether you use a pen name or your real name.

You just have to copyright your book in your local copyright office using both your pen name and your real name, or just your real name if you are not using a pseudonym. Then you get a certificate proving that you are the author of that piece showing your pen name and / or your real name. From that moment you can happily hide behind your pen name during all the publishing processes, like registrations or contacting professionals that will help you with the book. This should be done just after your book has been copy edited, so you register the final manuscript, including your book cover, with the copyright office.

When you fill in the form it is very important that you specify clearly both names, for example: (real name – John Thomas) (pen name – Maximo Kovak).

- In the UK: (cost £39) www.copyrightservice.co.uk/
- In the USA: (cost $35) www.copyright.gov
- In Spain: (cost €15) www.mcu.es/propiedadInt/CE/Registro Propiedad/ImpresosSolicitud.html
- Other options: (cost €40 per year) www.safecreative.org

Applying for tax exemption in the USA

Most self-publishing companies available right now are USA based. When you publish though them your book will be available for the USA market, but also people in Europe and other areas have access to your book. For authors wanting to publish via CreateSpace, read the following information carefully.

Did you know that USA will charge you 30% tax on each book you sell in the USA unless you apply for tax exemption in that country? This 30% will be deducted automatically from your royalties in CreateSpace.

Yes, I know, a total blast!

I got absolutely mad after reading dozens of blogs where people post questions related to tax exemption for non-USA citizens or USA citizens abroad. It was impossible to get a proper and organised answer explaining the process to follow step by step. it took me a very long time to find out how to do it properly.

Based on my experience applying for tax exemption in the USA, I describe below the two options you can follow to do your paperwork.

The two ways to apply for tax exemption:

1. **The lazy way.** Paying for the services of an agency approved by the IRS that will help you to sort out all the paperwork. The charge for this is around £450 and the time it takes to process is the same as if you do it yourself. You can find agents using the link below: http://www.irs.gov/Individuals/Acceptance-Agent-Program
2. **Do it yourself.** This way will save you a lot of money, but you need to be organised and read all the instructions carefully. If you make any mistakes your application might be refused and you will have to apply again, which might delay your publication date by several months. Follow the instructions below to learn how to do it yourself.

Why should I apply for tax exemption (tax treaty benefits)?
Because otherwise you will be charged 30% for any book sold in the USA territory. Many countries benefit from a treaty with the USA that reduces that tax rate, for example the rate for UK residents is 0%. If you are a USA citizen resident in another country you will also have to apply for tax exemption. Here are some common tax withholding rates by country, which are subject to change without notice:

- Canada: 0%
- Australia: 5%
- UK: 0%
- Japan: 0%
- India: 15%
- Spain: 10%

For more information about other countries, see tax treaty tables, page 38 at: www.irs.gov/pub/irs-pdf/p515.pdf

Things To Do and Consider Before Self-Publishing

This form is updated yearly so if the link does not work go to http://www.irs.gov/ and search for: Withholding of Tax on Non-resident Aliens and Foreign Entities pdf.

The process to apply for tax exemption is very similar for most countries. I am resident in the UK, so I get a 0% rate. This is the step by step process to follow to get your tax exemption.

Non USA citizens, individuals and business (employers) To simplify, this option is for people or corporations that will act as employers.	**Documents:** SS-4 form Commitment letter Certified copy of your passport W-8BEN non-individuals form	**Step1.** To get your taxpayer identification number (TIN) or EIN (for businesses) using the SS-4 form. You need to apply to the IRS in the USA, or any IRS office near you. **Step2.** Provide CreateSpace with the W-8BEN non-individuals form to stop them withholding your tax.
Non USA citizens, individuals. Authors that work individually, not as a business or corporation.	**Documents:** W7 form Commitment letter Certified copy of your passport W-8BEN individuals form	**Step1.** To get your (ITIN) number using the W7 form. You need to apply to the IRS in the USA, or any IRS office near you. **Step2.** Provide CreateSpace with the W-8BEN individuals form to stop them withholding your tax.
USA citizens living abroad.	**Documents:** Your SSN (Social Security number) W9 form	All USA citizens or residents in the country have an SSN. You have to provide this number to CreateSpace, with a W9 form.

When is the right moment to apply?

The process of applying for tax exemption is complex and takes about two to three months (if you do not make any mistakes) so you should start applying as soon as possible. You have to apply to the IRS (USA tax office). Once you've finished and reviewed your book, and while your book is being copy edited, you should start applying for tax exemption immediately.

Where can I get the forms from?

Go to the IRS website and type in the top search box the name of the form you are looking for. (www.irs.gov)

Where can I get the commitment letter sample from?

Most authors are struggling trying to find the right forms and examples of how to fill them in. Below I explain different ways in which you can get them fast.

The commitment letter is required to explain to the IRS why you want to apply for tax exemption. The website you are going to publish through (CreateSpace, for example) should provide the commitment sample letter. Without this letter your application to the IRS will be refused.

- Open the CreateSpace website (www.CreateSpace.com) and, using the search site tool, search for "Tax information". A document will appear explaining the procedures and at the bottom the letter and sample forms.
- If all this fails you will have to write to CreateSpace direct and ask them to forward you the forms and the letter.

I know, all this seems to be crazy. No one understands why CreateSpace makes the process so difficult, but the truth is that if you want to publish with them and have your book in Amazon without being charged 30%, you will have to go through the process and be patient. They constantly change the pages and links, so contact them direct with your questions and they will reply, normally within 48 hours. Having some Valium pills nearby could be very handy during this process.

I finally got the forms, but I'm still unsure how to fill them in.
It is very important you don't make any mistakes when filling in the forms, otherwise they will be rejected by the IRS. The CreateSpace link provided above has example forms, and explains how to correctly fill them in. If you cannot find examples of forms that are already filled in, I would suggest you call the closest IRS office and ask them for assistance. Some USA embassies have an IRS office inside.
http://www.irs.gov/uac/Contact-My-Local-Office-Internationally
It took me two days to be able to get hold of them; you have to be patient and keep trying. Have your questions written down, ready to ask. They are very helpful once you get to speak with them.

Each country has a different treaty, therefore the answers and boxes to tick are different.

Example guide to fill the forms for UK Residents.
I could not possibly give the answers for all countries as each one has a different treaty and therefore the answers on the forms vary, but here is an example used for UK residents that will help you to understand how to fill in the forms. It is nearly the same for other countries.

Individuals requesting tax treaty benefits and an ITIN (Individual Tax Identification Number) will be asked to provide:

At the IRS office:
1. The W7 form filled in correctly.
2. The commitment letter.
3. A certified colour copy of your passport or driving licence.

Once you get your ITIN tax number you must contact the website you are using for publishing your book, e.g. CreateSpace:
4. W-8BEN form properly filled in.

Self-Publishing

From the moment you apply to completion, when you get your ITIN, the whole process takes about eight weeks.

W7 form Fill in the form by hand.	Tick exception box (a)	Non-resident alien required to get ITIN to obtain tax treaty benefit
	Tick exception box (h) other	Write in the space provided "Id exception"
	Enter treaty country	Write "UK"
	Treaty article number	Write "article 12"
	Name section	Use your real name, not your pen name
	Your address	Your resident address
	You identification details	Passport or driving licence details
	Section 6a Country of citizenship	UK
	Section 6e have you ever received a ITIN number before?	No
	Signature / date / phone	Don't forget to sign, date, and include your phone number
Commitment letter. This letter is provided by the company you are publishing with, e.g. CreateSpace. This letter is directed to you; however, it explains to the IRS the reasons why you are applying for an ITIN. Without that letter, your application won't be accepted.	The publishing company you are using (Createspace, for example) should provide you with a letter template that includes: - Their company name. - Space to fill in the date and your name. - Explanation of why you have to apply for an ITIN. - Their signature.	The only thing you have to do is to print that letter then put the date and your full name in the spaces provided. Ideally the W7 form and the commitment letter should have the same date.

Passport certification	The easy and cheaper way.	If you are lucky enough to live in a city where the USA embassy has an IRS office, like in London, you can pop in with your form, letter and a **colour** copy of your passport, plus the original. The IRS office will stamp and certify the copy for you free of charge. I would suggest you don't take any electronic devices or phones with you when you visit the USA embassy. They are very strict about security and you will have a smoother entrance if you don't take any such devices with you.
	Option 1. Take the documents and originals to the IRS office yourself.	
	Option 2. Send the documents and the original identification document by post.	If you live too far away from an IRS office to call in, then you can post all the documents requested to the closest IRS office, with your original passport. You will have to provide a stamped, self-addressed envelope to get your passport returned. They will send back your passport soon after they receive your application

Self-Publishing

	Option 3. The more expensive way.	If you do not want to send your original documents to the IRS office, then you will have to get a notary to certify your passport copy. That will cost you about £80. The certified copy also has to be stamped by your embassy or the Home Office, otherwise they might refuse your application. After that you can send it with your other documents to the closest IRS office.
W-8BEN form for individuals Once you get your ITIN, you have to fill in the W-8BEN form and send it to the company that distributes your book, including your member ID number on the top of the form: **CreateSpace** c/o Vendor Maintenance PO Box 80683 Seattle, WA 98108-0683 **Smashwords, Inc.** Attn: Tax Compliance Dept. PO Box 11817 Bainbridge Island, WA USA 98110	Section 1: your name	Write your full real name, not your pen name.
	Section 2: county of incorporation or organization	N/A
	Section3: type of beneficial owner	Tick box (individual)
	Section 4: your address	Write your full residence address
	Section 6: US identification tax payer number	Write your ITIN number and tick box (ITIN)
	Section 9: Claim of tax treaty benefits	Tick box (a) and write the country you are resident in. Tick box (b)
	Signature / date / capacity	Sign. Write date. Capacity in which acting: write "self".

You need to allow two weeks from the day you post the form for the process to be completed. From that time, you will be entitled to tax treaty benefits and the distributor won't withhold the 30% tax anymore.

For individuals (employers) or businesses requesting tax treaty benefits and an EIN (Employer Identification Number), you will be asked to provide:

At the IRS office:
1. The SS-4 form filled in correctly.
2. The commitment letter
3. A certified colour copy of your passport or driving licence.

At CreateSpace:
1. W-8BEN form, properly filled in.

From the moment you apply, to completion, when you get your EIN, the process takes about eight weeks.

SS-4 FORM This example is for individuals acting as employers. If you are filing the form as a business or corporation, the boxes to tick will be different depending on the type of company you have.	Section 1 Legal name or entity (or individual) for whom the EIN is being requested.	**(Your full name)** as individual employer (or if you are applying as a business or corporation you have to write your company name here)
	Section 4a and 4b	**Your address**
	Section 7a Name of responsible party	**Your full name** (not the company name)
	Section 8a	Tick "no" (if you are an individual)
	Section 9a Type of entity	**Tick first box** "A sole proprietor" SSN
	Section 10 Reason for applying	**Tick box 3** Compliance with IRS regulations **Tick box 4** other:

Self-Publishing

		To obtain a reduction of withholding imposed by section 1441 pursuant to an income tax treaty.
	Section 18	Tick "no"
	Signature and date	Sign and date the form
Passport certification	Same process as for individuals (non-employers)	
W-8BEN form for individuals or companies (employers) The form is the same but the answers in this case are different, as it is not for individuals but for employers and companies. Once you get your EIN you must fill in the W-8BEN form and send it to the company that distributes your book: **CreateSpace** c/o Vendor Maintenance PO Box 80683 Seattle, WA 98108-0683 **Smashwords, Inc.** Attn: Tax Compliance Dept. PO Box 11817 Bainbridge Island, WA USA 98110	Section 1: name of individual or organization	You write here your name, as individual employer, or the name of your company.
	Section 2 :	Write your country
	Section 3:	Tick box "corporation"
	Section 4:	Address, postcode and country
	Section 6:	Write your EIN and tick box (EIN)
	Section 9:	Tick box "a" and write your country Tick also boxes "b" and "c"
	Signature / date / capacity	Sign. Write date. Capacity in which acting: write "self"

Getting your ISBN numbers.

What is an ISBN number?

This is a 10 or 13 digit number that is used to identify a particular book. The main purpose is to establish and identify one title or edition of a title from any given publisher. The ISBN itself has embedded meaning. There is a group or country identifier; a publisher identifier, a title identifier and the final digit in an ISBN will validate the ISBN. One thing I want everyone to focus on is the part that covers the publisher identifier.

When you get a "free" ISBN from places such as Smashwords or CreateSpace, they are the publisher, not you. Accepting their free ISBN will save you some headaches; however, if for any reason you have a problem with one of these companies and you wish to distribute your book via other outlets they won't allow you to use their ISBN number and you will have to get a new one.

For authors who wish only to publish one book, the free ISBN number might work, but for authors who feel writing is their thing and they might publish more than one book per year then I would suggest you get your own ISBN numbers.

Using a free CreateSpace or Smashwords ISBN:

Most CreateSpace (CS) books are Amazon owned, which means the author is using an Amazon CreateSpace ISBN, not their own ISBN purchased from an agent. That ISBN identifies the book as being a CreateSpace product. CreateSpace is the publisher on record.

This option is advisable if you want to hide that the book was self-published via Amazon and so perhaps avoid the stigma of that.

The ISBN belongs to CreateSpace, therefore the book publisher on record is CreateSpace. The author retains copyright of the book content itself, but the actual soft cover book form belongs to CreateSpace, probably along with any CS provided cover. The author could take the original book file to another company to produce another version of the book, but under a different ISBN. This is not appropriate and can cause confusion.

Using your own ISBN:

You can form your own publishing company to purchase your own ISBNs from an agent and use them for your books.

Owning your own ISBN is not that important if you are using only Amazon for printing and sales. If, however, you think booksellers or libraries would want your book or you are publishing your book on different websites, you'll need to read the article about Lightning Source regarding distribution and owning your own ISBN.

Having your own ISBN will save you problems if you decide to remove your book from Amazon and publish it on other websites. As you own the ISBN number, you are the publisher, and you will be able to publish that book using the same ISBN anywhere else.

Do I have to register a company before getting my ISBN?

Ideally you should, but it is not strictly necessary at that stage, unless you know for sure your book will sell one million copies during the first six months. By getting your own ISBN numbers you are registering as a publisher. You have the control and your info will be encoded in the ISBN number. When people scan your barcode, including the ISBN, they will know who is the company or publisher.

On the other hand, you are supposed to declare the income you earn as a publisher in your country and for your sales abroad, therefore you should be either a registered freelance or a company. You can be cheeky and register later on, but at this stage you will need to be clear about whether you want to be one or the other and – most importantly – what name you will be using. You will be asked to provide this information to the ISBN agency.

Where can I get an ISBN?

ISBNs are assigned to publishers in the country where the publisher's main office is based. This is irrespective of the language of the publication or the intended market for the book.

For example, The ISBN Agency is the national agency for the UK

Things To Do and Consider Before Self-Publishing

and Republic of Ireland. Publishers based elsewhere will not be able to get numbers from the UK Agency (even if they are British citizens).

Each country has different agencies which provide ISBNs. Go to Google and type "ISBN agency in (the name of your country)". You will find easily the agency responsible and you can speak with or email them to get the details and the forms required to apply for the numbers.

Who is eligible for ISBNs?
Any publisher who is publishing a qualifying product for general sale or distribution to the market. By "publishing", we mean making a work available to the public.

What is a publisher?
The publisher is generally the person or body who takes the financial risk in making a product available. For example, if a product went on sale and sold no copies at all, the publisher is usually the person or body who loses money. If you get paid anyway, you are likely to be a designer, printer, author or consultant of some kind.

You don't need to be registered as a publisher when you apply for your ISBNs; however, you will need to register later to pay tax and declare your earnings. The ISBN agency will ask you to provide information like; publisher's name, trim size of the book, book price per edition, formats the book will be published in, etc.

How long does it take to get an ISBN?
In the UK, the standard service time is ten working days. This excludes weekends, Bank Holidays and days when the office is closed. There is also a Fast-track service, which is a three working day processing period, but it is more expensive. The processing period begins when a correctly completed application is received in the ISBN Agency, not when it is posted.

How much does it cost to get an ISBN?

ISBNs	10 day delivery	Fast-track 3 day delivery
10 ISBNs	£126	£199
100 ISBNs	£294	£360

CreateSpace offers you one ISBN for $90, but you can get 10 ISBNs for not much more when you order in advance through an agency.

How many ISBNs do I need for my book?

You will need one ISBN for your paperback edition and other for your e-book edition.

This question is regularly discussed in forums and people seem to offer different answers. You are supposed to get an ISBN number for each format the book is published in, but as the self-publishing market is still not fully regulated, that is not always the case.

Smashwords offers authors different e-book formats: epub, pdf, Kindle, RTF, LRF, etc.; however, they will ask you for just one ISBN to use for all formats. When you publish through CreateSpace you will need another ISBN for your print edition.

On the other hand, if your book is published in English but later you decide to translate it into another language, you will need two new ISBNs for that edition. If you bought ten ISBNs, you will be using four for that book in total. For example:

ISBN 978-0-9475953-0-9	E-book English edition	E-book price £2.99
ISBN 978-0-9375953-0-9	Paperback English edition	Book price £4.99
ISBN 978-0-9675953-0-9	E-book Spanish edition	E-book price €3.99
ISBN 978-0-9175953-0-9	Paperback Spanish edition	Book price €6.99

Getting your barcode for your print edition.

After obtaining your ISBNs, if you have decided to publish a print edition of your book, you can order your barcode. You have to provide the barcode to the designer who is creating your book cover design and he will insert it on the back cover.

If you are publishing using CreateSpace you won't need to get your own barcode. CreateSpace will place a 90000 price barcode extension, which is acceptable to Amazon and all the EDC channel partners. It will be read properly by barcode scanners, but basically translates to "no price encoded". Many self-publishing authors prefer that, because if the price was encoded and they wanted to change it down the road, then they'd have to revise the cover file and resubmit.

In this case, ask your cover designer to leave the space for the barcode empty.

Why publishers should use barcodes

Barcode scanning is the fastest and most accurate way for retailers to collect the information they need about the products they are selling. All major bookshops operate electronic point of sale (EPOS) systems which enable them to maximise sales and reduce stocks using the sales information they have collected. To enable full use of this equipment, it is essential for publishers to follow the required trade standards for the use of barcodes on books.

Publishers that do not barcode their titles may well find retailers refusing to accept their publications.

Publishers of all sizes will get direct or indirect benefits from barcoding:

- The barcodes can be scanned during distribution to ensure accurate servicing to booksellers.
- Retail scanning allows retailers to re-order stock so that a title can be readily on display.

Self-Publishing

What is a barcode?

A barcode is a rectangular block of parallel bars and light spaces, arranged in a particular format, to meet specific requirements. It is a conversion of eye readable information into machine readable form.

Within the book industry, a barcode contains a book's International Standard Book Number (ISBN), which since 1 January 2007 comprises 13 digits (12 digits plus a check digit), with the option of including one other piece of supplementary information, such as the price or stock code for in-house use.

The machine readable code is a structured symbol containing three main elements.

The EAN13 barcode forms the main part with, below the code, an eye readable version of the 13-digit number. Publishers may also wish to print, above the code, an eye readable version of the ISBN retaining the hyphenation structure of the number.

A publisher using a third party distributor should consult the distributor when selecting the most suitable version of the bar code.

Recommended barcode symbols

Version NR

The basic symbol includes the ISBN in EAN barcode form and in eye readable font above the code. This version provides all the information needed by UK retailers and is generally recommended for use in the UK book trade.

Sizes
34 x 29mm
36 x 30mm
38x 31mm
40 x 33mm
42 x 34mm

Version NK (with price add-on)

The expanded symbol includes the ISBN in EAN barcode and encodes the price in a supplementary barcode. UK publishers are recommended to use this version with the US price if they are selling a book into the US market. In the UK, booksellers use the basic symbol to look up on their EPOS systems the price relating to the encoded ISBN, whereas in the US an encoded price is required by some retailers. The presence of a US price is not an impediment to the correct reading of the barcode by UK retailers.

Sizes
50 x 29mm
53 x 30mm
56 x 31mm
58 x 33mm
61 x 34mm

The currency the price is in is identified by the initial digit of the add-on code. The 5 digit supplementary, shown in the example, enables prices between 1p (00001) and £99.99 (09999) to be machine readable. The current allocations of currency prefix digits for English language publishing is as follows:

0   UK £ price to £99.99
5   US $ price to $99.99
6   Canadian $ price to $99.99

Prefixes 1, 2, 3 and 4 are also reserved for use in the USA for books at higher prices.

Size and location of barcodes

The size of the ISBN / EAN barcode is dependent upon the version used and magnification. The nominal magnification is referred to as 100%. Most good quality print techniques may produce sufficiently consistent symbols to allow for the symbol magnification to be below 100%.

Self-Publishing

The smallest allowable size is 80% magnification, but this greatly reduces the print tolerances available and should only be considered where space is at a high premium. Flexography and silk screen processes may require symbols to be magnified greater than 100%. The maximum size symbol is at 200% magnification. The height of the barcode is an essential aspect to ensure that it can be scanned first time on all types of scanner. Truncation – shortening of the height of the bar code – should be avoided. If there is a real need to truncate the symbol, this should be kept to a minimum.

The preferred position for the ISBN / EAN13 symbol is the bottom right-hand corner of the back of the book cover or jacket. The same ruling also applies to slip cases, boxed sets, paperbacks, books with printed covers and directly printed labels.

The preferred position assists speedy operational use in bookshops or warehouses since staff can rely on finding symbols in one standard position.

As the symbol must be situated on a smooth surface, it is recommended that no part of the symbol and light margins should be closer than 6mm to the edge of the wrapper / cover, or the crease where the cover is shaped over the spine.

The light margins to the left and right of the symbol (a space of approximately 2.5mm at nominal size) are vital to ensure that the barcode is scannable. Additionally, the printed symbol must not be obscured by, for example, the use of promotional bands wrapped round the jacket. If the symbol has been manufactured to the approved standards, shrink-wrapping does not normally present problems when being scanned.

Formatting your book

You will need to find professionals that will format your book for your e-book edition and also for your paperback edition.

E-book formatting

Each website (Smashwords, CreateSpace, etc.) has its own specific guidelines and rules related to formatting. When you get a professional to do the formatting for your e-book, tell him / her what company you are using to publish your so they will deliver a final copy that follows their guidelines and will be easy to upload on the site you will use. At this stage, and before you contact the formatter, I would suggest you check copyright page examples. This is the page that normally is at the front of most books and includes the copyright info, disclaimers, ISBN numbers, etc. Remember that if you got your own ISBN, you are the publisher, so you are not obliged to put "published by ..." Smashwords or CreateSpace. See example below.

FIRST FLOOR – ROOM 16

Maximo Kovak

Published by Maximo Kovak

Smashwords Edition
Copyright © 2013 Maximo Kovak
Copyright registration number 284666398

www.maximokovak.com
All rights reserved

First Digital Edition, 2013

ISBN: 978-0-9575953-2-3 (E-book)
ISBN: 978-0-9575953-0-9 (Paperback)

Smashwords Edition, License Notes

This e-book is licensed for your personal enjoyment only. This e-book may not be re-sold or given away to other people. If you would like to share this book with another person, please purchase an additional copy for each recipient. If you're reading this book and did not purchase it, or it was not purchased for your use only, then please return to Smashwords.com and purchase your own copy. Thank you for respecting the hard work of the author.

Disclaimer

The author, who decided to keep himself anonymous, portrays his experiences as a male escort whilst living in London. All the names and locations have been changed to make sure real characters in the book won't be recognised. Any resemblance to any person is purely coincidental, although some aspects of the characters may have been inspired by some persons I actually know and admire. Cover: The model on the cover is not an escort or the author. The author holds the rights for the use of that image.

Print edition formatting

The formatting for a print edition is very different to that required for an e-book, therefore you will need to get a professional to do that for you. At this point you have to take decisions related to the formatting design. Type of layout, fonts you prefer for titles and other text, type of decoration to use in between scenes or at the end of each chapter, etc.

Most professional formatters will send you options before starting the process so you can discuss details with them. Make sure you are clear about what you want from the beginning so you avoid possible misunderstandings.

Creating your marketing plan.

Start your marketing before you write the book.

The best time to design and implement your marketing plan of action is *before* you even start writing your book. It takes time to build relationships, learn what your readers want and need, and develop a base of rabid fans that clamour for more.

Grow your readership as you write your book, and when it's time to launch your baby, you'll already have an invested and eager audience waiting.

Even if you already have your book in hand, don't panic! The process is still the same. It just may take a little longer to see the book sales come rolling in.

- **Focus more on discoverability than selling.** Your work is important, so help those who can benefit from it to find it.
- **Accept responsibility for the marketing and promotion of your book.** Even if you choose to outsource some of the work, your book's success depends on you taking action.
- **Marketing and promotion is just an extension of your author platform.** The lines between platform building and book marketing are often blurred.

You will find later on in this book some useful ideas to promote your books in the "Marketing your book" section.

Self-Publishing

Before publishing checklist

Finish your book	✓
Put the book in a drawer for a couple of weeks / take a break	2 weeks
Choose a title for your book	1 day
Choose your pen name or author's name	1 day
Book cover ideas / first draft	2 days
Review your book and make the final version of the manuscript	1 week
Copy edit your book	1-2 months
Synopsis and book description	2 days
Get a cover designer / final cover for print edition, including the barcode space	1 week
Copyright the final manuscript, when already copy edited plus the book cover	1-2 weeks
Apply for tax exemption in the USA	2 months
Apply for your ISBNs, if required	3-10 days
Book formatting for e-book version	1 or 2 weeks
Book formatting for print version	2 or 3 weeks
Get your barcode for the print edition (if you wish)	5 days
Create your marketing plan.	1 week
Total time to get ready your book for publishing	**5 to 7 months**

CHAPTER TWO

Publishing Your Book

My book was ready for publishing. I was so excited when this moment arrived. I had everything ready: the book had been copy edited, and formatted for both paperback and e-book editions; my ISBN and tax forms had been sent, the cover had been professionally designed; and I had my barcode. Finally I could publish my book and rest.

Nooooooooooo, very far from the truth. Your work as author and self-publisher never ends!!!

Once your book is ready, you will have to complete the registration process on the websites which will sell your book, fill in many forms online, enter information, and upload your book for approval.

During this process you have to be very careful. Again, many questions will come up and most probably you will feel anxious.

You are nearly there!! You want your book to be out and available for the world to see, and for it to start selling straight away! Well, slow down! If you make mistakes during this process your book will be rejected, which will delay your publication. Read very carefully all the steps and undertake the process slowly. Most of the information they will ask you for, you will know already if you have followed the pre-process for self-publishing I explained to you earlier.

CHAPTER THREE

Submitting Your Book

You will need to fill in different sections:

Author's details: In this section you will enter your pen name (if you are using one) or your real name as author, your address and other details.

Your publisher / company and tax details: If you went along the route of getting your own ISBN number, you will already have registered as a publisher. If you have done your homework you should have your tax exemption ITIN number ready so you can get the treaty tax discount for non-USA citizens. Most websites give you the option to publish your book even if you don't have the ITIN number ready, but you will have to provide that info later, otherwise you will be charged 30% tax on top of their fees.

Your bank details: The bank account you will use to get your royalties paid into. Remember if you chose to be a company you will need a company bank account. To open a company account is more complex and might take from 1 to 3 weeks. If you are a freelance you can use a normal account for this section.

Your book details: Here you will be asked to insert a short book description and a more elaborate one. The title, the author's name, the tag keywords, trim size for your book, type of paper (for print edition) and to upload your book files, including the cover and your already copy edited and formatted manuscript. Each website has its own guidelines and rules for uploading files and accepting covers and manuscripts. If you decide to do your own cover design and book formatting you will have to be extremely careful and follow all their instructions, otherwise your book will be rejected. I saved time and headaches by paying professionals to do my cover and formatting. They delivered the files for me ready to upload, following the guides required, so the registration was smooth and the book was accepted at the first attempt.

Here we go! Your book has been submitted and accepted. You are probably feeling a rush of fulfilment and feeling very proud of yourself. If you got here, you should. Well done!

My book is already online and available, so can I relax now?

NO.

How do you expect people to learn about your book?

Do you think the sales will magically happen?

Every time you start or plan a new book you should also prepare your marketing plan for that specific book. This involves a certain amount of research and preparation prior to the book's submission. To have this marketing plan done before submitting is essential. Once your book is available you should start the promotion straight away. Sometimes the marketing starts even before your manuscript is available; for example, submitting your book for reviews in advance.

CHAPTER FOUR

Marketing Your Book

Your book is already on sale and available, but you still have a lot of work to do if you really want to sell more than a dozen books per month. You won't have big posters advertising your books in the main metro stations or a publisher that will make deals with the main bookshops, therefore you need to find solutions to let people know about your book.

Here you have a list of marketing ideas, choose the ones that suit you the best.

Choosing the right genre categories:

When you submit your book to the different websites, CreateSpace, Smashwords, Lulu, etc., you will be asked what categories you wish to include your book in. It is important you choose the right ones to make it easier for readers to find your book. On some websites, the categories and subcategories listings can be very confusing and long, but take your time going through the options. Here is an example of the main categories, but each one is subdivided into many other sub-categories. It would be too much to show them all here.

Self-Publishing

Fiction	Adventure
	African American
	Anthologies
	Children's Books
	Christian
	Drama
	Erotica
	Fantasy
	Gay & Lesbian
	Graphic Novels/Comics
	Historical
	Holiday
	Horror
	Humor & Comedy
	Literary
	Mystery & Detective
	Poetry
	Romance
	Science Fiction
	Sports
	Thriller & Suspense
	Western
	Women's Fiction
	Young Adult/Teen
Non Fiction	Biography
	Business & Economics
	Childrens' books
	Cooking
	Entertainment
	Health & Wellbeing
	History
	Inspiration
	Parenting
	Politics
	Reference
	Relationships and Family
	Religion
	Self Improvement
	Sports
	Travel

Marketing Your Book

Choosing the wrong category might affect your sales negatively. Most websites give you the option to change categories afterwards if you wish, but each time you make any changes in your book settings, they will need to be approved and this might take one or two days. During that period your book won't be available to the public.

Creating your own website

This is a very important marketing tool. Once your book is live you will start contacting people and you will need a place to provide them with info about your books and yourself. You want to give a professional impression to the media, readers and people who start contacting you. A bad website won't do you any favours, marketing wise.

Getting a website designer
If you don't have any knowledge about websites, I would recommend you get a professional to build the site for you; however, it will cost you more than if you do it yourself. Depending on the complexity of your site it might cost you anything between £400 and £1200. The more features and sections you add, the more it will cost. You will have to provide the following basic information to the web designer:

- The number of sections required and the title names for the menu.
- The sub-divisions or sub-sections.
- The visual or photos to be included on your website.
- The preferred colour scheme for the backgrounds, etc.

I would suggest looking at website templates online or at other authors' websites to get some ideas before you contact the designer. The more info and clarity you give to your designer, the easier will be his job and therefore the cheaper the cost. If you provide a website tree to him, even better. The website tree defines all the contents and sections on your website, click by click. Here is a basic example:

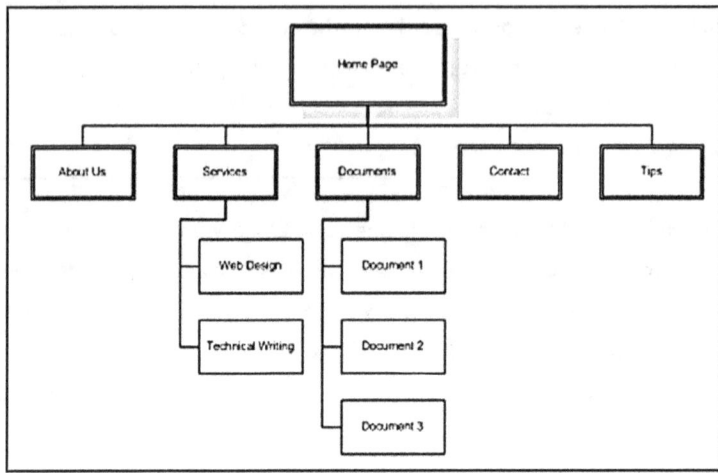

This way you can give clear guidelines to the designer and also it will be good for you to organise your thoughts and ideas.

You will have to add to the website tree the contents for each section and the main guidelines and ideas for the design. For example:

Main Guidelines	1- I would like to have an elegant but contemporary design using the colours red, white and grey through the website. I don't want a flash intro. 2- I prefer HTML, so all devices can access my website. 3- I would like the website to be compatible with the main browsers like Firefox, Chrome, Explorer, Opera etc. 4- See templates example link below www.maximokovak.com	
Home page	Text for home page	Visuals to add in home page
Products	Text to add in this section	Visuals to use here
Services	Text for services section	Visuals to add here
Email accounts to create	contact@petersocha.com	social@petersocha.com

Your emails: I would suggest you get at least two email addresses, one for your contact form and general enquires, and another to use on social networks. You won't want your main email bombarded by email from Facebook or Twitter, so better to create a separate one just for that. The web designer will set up the accounts for you using your hosting service.

SEO: Once your website is completed you should engage a specialist in search engine optimization (SEO). This professional will do the basic work necessary to make sure your website is visible to the main search engines, like Google, Yahoo, etc. You might have the most beautiful and interesting website in the world, but without good SEO no one will see you!!!

Where do I find the professionals? Well, there are many websites where you can find professionals, like Peopleperhour, or you can search on Google. It won't be difficult to find someone. Make sure you get more than one quote. Do not say yes to the first applicant, and check his portfolio and experience first. Also check their availability and work load over the next few weeks. Freelancers sometimes take several jobs at the same time, but they won't inform their clients if they do not ask. You will probably have to wait a long time before they finish your job if that is the case.

How do payments work? You should never pay the full amount in advance. You can expect to pay 10% or 20% in advance and then the rest after completion. Always get an invoice, as you might need to justify your expenses for tax purposes later on.

Building the website yourself:
This option could save you a lot of money, but it is recommended only for people who have clear knowledge about website design, or at least have some of the following skills:

- Knowledge about hosting
- Website templates
- CMS
- SEO
- Email accounts set up
- Photoshop

The first things to do are:

Buy your domain: e.g. www.maximokovak.com You might chose to buy other domain names like .net, .info, .co.uk, etc., so no one can create a similar website using your name. However, that will cost you much more money. If you don't think you will become super famous, then buy just one domain. Another thing to consider is the privacy of your personal data. If you are using a pseudonym and you don't want your real name to come out as owner of the website, then you should make your personal details private. All hosting services provide that option, at a cost.

If you are creating an author page, you'd better use your author name for your domain. If you are creating a business page, then use your business name as the domain; or if you are creating a book page, then use the name of the book or an abbreviated form of the title. You will want to find a domain name that is short, simple and related to the purpose of your page.

Buy your hosting: This is the space where your website will be hosted. Google "website hosting" services and choose the most convenient for you. For small websites you won't need professional hosting, just a basic or medium package. Compare and read carefully before buying anything.

Buying your own website template: If you don't want to build your website from scratch you can easily buy a website template, with

CMS, and adapt it to your needs and requirements. Using the CMS you can change the colours, text, sections, pages, etc.

Creating your email accounts: Using your hosting account, you can create your own emails. Most hosting packages provide a number of free email accounts.

SEO: It is highly recommended you do the basic SEO for your website or get someone to do it for you, for the reasons mentioned before.

Text and visuals: Take some time to work on the contents of your website. People will read what you write, so think twice about the contents. Short and appealing is much better than long and boring, text wise. You can get your visuals from Google images, or you can buy your images from photo stock websites. Remember, your website is the main door for your audience, readers, the media and people wanting to know about you. First impressions count!

Getting a web designer	Designer fee £400 – £1200 Hosting £60 – £90 Domain £20 SEO £40
Doing it yourself	Website template £60 – £100 Hosting £60 – £90 Domain £20 SEO £40

Website contents

I am not a web designer, but I have built more than twenty websites for my projects and I have worked many times on website content development. We are in a visual era, where most people are constantly bombarded by visuals and information: iPhones, iPads, TV, YouTube,

Facebook, cinema, websites, radio, printed adverts, etc. This constant flood of images and information makes people more impatient and that is the reason why if they don't get attracted by your home page during the first 10 seconds then they are already gone.

Home page: Your website home page should be appealing, with eye-catching colours, more visuals than text, and a very well organised and easy to use menu or menus. Your "contact me" button is the ultimate and most important tool on any author's website and it should be right in front of your eyes and visible. Your home page will be the door to as many other sections as you want to create. I am not here to tell you how your website should be, but let me suggest some options based on what most authors use:

> **About me:** Most readers love to know personal details about the people who write the books they are reading. Satisfying the reader's curiosity, letting them know who is the person behind the book, will draw them closer to you.
> **Reviews:** Show in this section the best reviews you've got so far or even write your own reviews of books you have read lately, giving your audience some idea about what you enjoy reading.
> **News and events:** This section is open to any news related to your career as author: book signings, new releases, conferences, etc.
> **Blog:** Why not create your own blog on your website? This is a great way to get potential loyal followers.
> **Books:** This section can be used to provide full profiles about your latest book releases. Please, do not bother readers with huge text descriptions. Make it short and appealing. Include the cover visuals and, most importantly, the links to where they can buy each book.
> **Contact me:** The most important button on your whole website. The main aim for any author is to create an audience

Marketing Your Book

and a group of loyal followers. Spending time answering your readers' questions or any queries from the media is very important if you wish to become a successful author.

Follow me: This section is very important too and should include the links to your Facebook, Twitter and LinkedIn pages. The more people following, you the better.

Making your website more interactive

Build your website address into your book.
When writing your book, include as many reasons as possible for readers to visit your website. Success requires more than simply listing your website address in your biography or on the last page of the book.

Give readers valid reasons to visit your site. Offer downloadable versions of reader engagement tools like checklists and worksheets. Promise updated content and new information, such as ideas and topics that occurred to you after you completed your book

Don't view your website strictly as a promotional tool. Instead, view it as a "service" or resource intended to help readers make the most of your book.

Encourage reader comments and questions.
Use your website to create an interactive relationship with your readers. Solicit their comments and questions. Offer a prize for the best question of the month and answer the question on your website's home page. Respond to reader emails as quickly as possible. If their comments are critical, create a dialogue and try to understand the criticism from your reader's point of view. You'll likely gain new information and ideas that you would otherwise never encounter.

Offer information to the media.
Create a "press room" where members of the media can download files containing scanned images of you, as well as the front cover(s) of

your book(s). Scanned images which can be immediately downloaded make your book(s) more attractive to reviewers and other writers.

Include a "backgrounder" describing you and your firm's background as well as your personal side. Include information that emphasises the timeliness of your book and its importance to your readers. Provide answers to frequently asked questions.

Publish an email newsletter.
You can do your readers a favour, as well as maintain your awareness and pre-sell your next book, by publishing an email newsletter. Make your email newsletter as genuinely helpful as possible. Instead of a long, infrequently published newsletter, offer short nuggets of information that appear on a regular basis. Readers are busy and will respond favourably to concise, easily digested information.

When soliciting reader email addresses, always include your privacy statement, which should state that you will never rent, sell or share your readers' email addresses. And make sure you live up to your promise!

These sections are the basic ones, but the more innovative and creative you are, the more appealing your website will be.

Targeting audience

Self-publishers – especially non-fiction authors – give themselves the best chance of success by focusing on how they will market a book before they write it. Why? How your book addresses the basic questions of the readers you hope to sell it to will be crucial to how well it's received in the marketplace.

If you want to sell books, you need to know who is buying them.

The Planning Process
1. Break your markets into groups (segment).
2. Choose the group(s) that are going to be your best customers (target).

3. Learn how, when, where, and why they buy books, and be there when they are (intercept).
4. Create a special marketing mix (product, price, promotions, and distribution) for each target group (position).
5. Create a "to do" list and turn it into a "to sell" list.

This may seem complicated, but it is not. If you do it once, you will see how simple it is. Let me just give you an example of steps 1 and 2 to get you started.

1. **Break your market into groups.** Do not try to be all things to all buyers. Look for groups that "buy and use" similarly. I asked my friend, who owns a sex shop, which are your main market groups. He said: We have identified three main ones; women who buy toys and gear for themselves, men who buy toys and gear for the ladies; and, finally, the gay consumers. The biggest spenders are the gay consumers, as they don't have kids and they have more cash to spend on extras, therefore we decided to target them and focused our marketing on that group.

2. **Choose your target markets.** Of all the groups you identify, you cannot possibly afford the time and money to market to all of them. Choose your top markets. My latest book was an erotic gay memoir. I knew my markets were the gay community, people connected to the book's themes, male bisexual or curious, and perhaps some women interested in gay related subjects. The easiest and most prominent market was the gay community. I focused all my efforts on targeting them as potential clients, rather than spreading my marketing activity and trying to target all the possible groups.

Self-Publishing

Each book will have a different target audience. It is very important you identify the groups you want to target or the type of people that might be interested in your book. This will be very helpful, enabling you to direct your marketing strategy toward the right sectors. As I previously said, the target audience for my book "First Floor Room 16" was mostly the gay and lesbian community, therefore, I made a plan directed at this group:

1. Social media directed to gay and lesbian users.
2. Search of magazines and newspapers for gay readers.
3. Selection of organizations and charities related to the book's subject.
4. Reading groups related to my subject.
5. Listing of friends and relatives connected to my target group to spread the word.
6. Specialised bookshops selling books related to my theme.
7. Blogging on LGBT blogs.
8. Visuals and text on my website directed at my target audience.
9. Marketing stationery directed at my main target audience.

Selling your book in independent bookshops

This is a road full of bumps and disappointments, but I understand many self-published authors might want to have their books physically on the shelves of real bookshops. If you do, here are some suggestions to make your encounter with the book store owners less unsatisfactory.

Big bookshops won't take self-published books, but small independent ones related to your book themes might consider stocking some copies.

I would advise you to contact them in person rather than via email.

When you speak with them, your approach should be humble but confident.

Marketing Your Book

Do some research and make a list of the independent bookshops you want to target, and select only the ones related to your book's theme. You will be wasting your time if you approach a bookshop specialising in childrens' books if your books are of an erotic adult nature. Find out if they have a website and do some research about their history, who are the owners or sales managers, and any other relevant info. Knowing about them might help you to sell your book when you speak directly with them.

When you visit them, take with you:

- Ten copies of your book for each bookshop.
- Your business card.
- Several receipt acknowledgement forms. These should be completed in duplicate, with one copy for you and the other to be kept by the bookshop. See example as follow.

MAXIMO KOVAK BOOKS　　　　　　　**Receipt Acknowledgement**
243 Thames Road
London SE10 5QJ
Office: 020 71 32 .....
contact@maximokovak.com

Company name and address	
Book title	
Number of copies held	
Price per copy	
Total	
Date	

Details for payment:
By cheque:
By bank transfer:

New copies can be ordered by email: contact@maximokovak.com
Please allow 10 days for delivery.

Self-Publishing

This receipt acknowledges the delivery of a number of copies for the bookshop named above.

The copies are held by the shop for sale. Once the copies are sold, the bookshop promises to make the payment using the payment details below. Any remaining copies unsold will be returned to the owner with no charge. If any of the unsold copies is damaged, the bookshop will be charged for that copy.

Contact full name	
Email address	
Contact number	

Negotiating the price: You should do your sums before approaching bookstores. This will help you to make a reasonable price proposal. Authors can get a discounted price when buying their own titles from print on demand companies (e.g. CreateSpace). I could get my book for a price of £3.50 per unit, so I decided to sell it to the shops for £6. I proposed they should use a retail price of £10 per unit, so they could make £4 profit per copy sold. I convinced two independent book stores to stock my book on their shelves using this system.

Dealing with disappointment: Do not expect all the bookshops you approach to receive you with open arms. You have to be prepared to deal with rejection and even very rude people. I had a very bad experience when visiting one of the bookshops on my target list. They treated me very badly, and basically the manager pointed to the door and asked me to leave the premises. Believe me, I had made a polite approach, so I could not understand why I was being treated in such a rude way when my only intention was to try to stock my book in their shop. The manager did not even allow me to finish my explanation before he threw me out. This experience did not stop me visiting other bookshops. Luckily I had a better welcome in other shops.

The follow up: The work does not stop after you've convinced the bookshop to stock a number of copies of your book; you will have to follow up and check after two months whether or not they need more copies. Make sure you keep all the receipts and information in a safe place at your office as you will need them later.

If the book is selling well, they might contact you asking for more copies. I would recommend not delivering more copies until the previous ones are paid for. For that you will have to send them an invoice.

Believe me, the route of stocking your book in bookshops is a hassle and very time consuming but, most importantly, you won't make much profit from it. However, if the temptation of having your book in real bookshops is tickling you, go for it – just be prepared for rejection and hard work.

Media and advertising

Press releases: Are you Stephen King or Dan Brown? No? Then the media won't be interested in your press releases. You can send hundreds of them, but they will go straight into the archives. Unless you have a very good contact at a newspaper / magazine or your book is related to very topical news, you won't get a mention or an article by using press releases.

My friends working in the media told me that they receive hundreds of press releases every month from self-published authors, and to that you have to add the other hundreds from publishers' PR agencies, trying to promote new authors or books.

Should you get a press release ready in case? Yes, but don't think it will magically bring you free advertising. You can post it on your website or keep it in case you get an interview in the future, or someone asks for it.

Sending your book to the media: I had the great idea to send a media pack to fifteen selected magazines. The pack included a paperback copy of my book, a press release and a presentation letter subtly asking for a mention or an article. Media packs are expensive, so I dedicated a lot of time to selecting the right magazines and newspapers, reading their websites, finding out the name of the person I should address it to and making sure they publish book reviews in their magazines. I was convinced they would feel flattered by me sending a free copy of my book and they would contact me, at least to say thank you or ask me some questions, opening the door to some mention or an article.

I DID NOT GET ONE SINGLE RESPONSE.

Paying for an advertisement: I decided to change my strategy and check out the cost of a paid advertisement in some of the magazines I'd sent the media pack to. I found out the name of the person in charge of advertising and emailed them asking for prices for a quarter page banner to publicise my book. I got a response from all of the magazines in hours! What bastards! I thought.

Well, this was my opportunity to play them at the same game, so I emailed them back explaining that their competitors had offered me a free full article about my book on a different week if I were to buy a quarter page banner. Suddenly I started to receive emails from them offering me more and more free things.

I now had them on their knees. I selected the best offers and spread them out over time so not all the adverts or articles came out at the same time. By paying for two banners in different magazines (£120 each) I gained nearly two months' of advertising coverage.

Week 1: paid banner in magazine A.
Week 2: free article about my book in magazine A.
Week 3: free mention in the magazine A newsletter (received by 5,000 users).
Week 4: paid advert in magazine B.
Week 5: free article / interview about the book on magazine B's website.
Week 6: free banner on magazine B's website.

During this process they all suddenly remembered my media pack and my book. Apparently it was in a drawer gathering dust but, as I was willing to pay some money, I rapidly became of interest to them. They even read my book and made some comments about it in their articles. What an honour!

I learnt the lesson the hard way. Media people are like vultures and to get to them you just have to provide the right bait.

Did my sales improve as a result of paying for advertisements? Only 5% to 10%, so I wouldn't say that it was a huge success. But the adverts created name awareness, which is quite important for new upcoming authors.

Book reviews and book contests

Getting reviews for your book is an excellent way to promote your new release(s) and gain credibility, but it is a difficult task.

First you need to submit your book to a reviewer, wait one to three weeks to see if you have been accepted and, if you have been, then wait two or three months to get your review online.

Of course, following this process does not guarantee a good review, but if you get one, it could be a great tool for marketing your book. Some places will consider your book if you send them the manuscript two or three months before publication only. Therefore you need to keep this in mind and submit your new book just after the copy editing is done.

Here are some useful e-book review links:

Kindle Obsessed
Link: www.kindleobsessed.com/review-request/
Kindle Obsessed is run by one Misty Baker, a voracious reader who enjoys dystopian literature (i.e. "Hunger Games") and paranormal-esque reading. She adores zombies and vampires and things that make you go gulp in the night.

On her review request page she claims to accept all genres, but I'm thinking it might be best to stick with the types of books she has featured on her site. In fact, check out what she's currently reading on her site before submitting.

After you send Misty details about your Kindle book, allow 72 hours for her to either give you the thumbs up *(yes, I'll review your book)*, or a thumbs down *(sorry, not my cup of tea)*. From there it could take anywhere from 1-3 months for your book review to be posted on her website.

Indie Author Book Reviews
Link: http://indieauthorbookreviews.wordpress.com/request-a-book-review/

Author Anne Chaconas runs the Indie Author Book reviews blog. She does book reviews and author interviews. She accepts guest bloggers and she'll even promote your giveaway. Reviews are posted on the Indie Author Book Reviews blog, Amazon, BN, Smashwords, Goodreads, LibraryThing and Shelfari. If your title is accepted for review, you'll be emailed within a week.

Preference is given to: general fiction, women's literature, chick lit, literary fiction, historical fiction, romance, thrillers, mysteries, dramas and young adult titles.

She may also consider: memoirs, biographies, humour, sci-fi, fantasy, horror and non-fiction.

Unless you're on a blog tour, reviews may take as long as 3-4 months to go live. For details about submitting your book for review, go to her website link.

Cath 'n' Kindle Book Reviews
Link: http://cnkbookreviews.blogspot.co.uk/

Cathy Speight enjoys reading everything except Christian fiction. What is "everything" exactly?

Well, according to the categories on her website, she has reviewed books in the following genres: chick lit, children's, contemporary, crime / thriller / mystery / suspense, dog fiction, erotica, historical, horror, humour, non-fiction, romance, sci-fi / fantasy, short stories, urban fantasy, women's fiction and young adult.

If you'd like Cathy to review your book, send her a private message on Facebook or email her at (cathyspeight54@hotmail.com).

Romancing the Book
Link: http://romancing-the-book.com/book-reviews

Romancing the Book is all about love, romance and everything in between. They review sub-genres like: adventure, adult themes, anthology, biography, chick lit, contemporary, fantasy, futuristic, historical, horror, inspiration, interracial, mystery, non-fiction, paranormal, sci-fi, steampunk, suspense, time travel, urban fantasy, western and young adult.

To get the ball rolling you'll need to submit information about your Kindle book on their website. If one of their reviewers is interested in reviewing it, they'll ask you for a review copy. A review of your Kindle book will appear on their site 4-6 weeks after you've submitted it.

Self-Publishing

Big Al's Books & Pals
Link: http://booksandpals.blogspot.co.uk/p/submitting-book-for-review.html

Hurray for Big Al's for focusing on indie (independent) authors who are Kindle (and Nook) published. His blog is a hotbed of review activity.

All genres of fiction and many segments of non-fiction are accepted here. Non-fiction must be targeted to a layperson – think travel narrative.

Kindle books submitted here may be reviewed up to a year after submission. Reviews will also be submitted to Amazon within two weeks after it's listed on the blog.

The Book Hookup
Link: http://thebookhookup.com/review-policy/

The Book Hookup is a consort of five book blogging ladies who span across North America. In addition to book reviews, they also host author interviews, guest bloggers and authors who are on blog tours.

They prefer e-books in the following genres: contemporary fiction, romance, historical romance, urban fantasy, dark fantasy, paranormal and young adult.

Book Lovers Inc.
Link: http://www.bookloversinc.com/review-policy/

If you're a self-published or vanity press author, Book Lovers Inc. ISN'T the site for you.

But if you're traditionally published and your genre centres around: fantasy, urban fantasy, romance, paranormal romance, historical fiction, speculative fiction or young adult, then you'll definitely want to submit your title to them. They prefer to receive review copies through NetGalley.

According to their website, it sounds like *a good number* of submitted titles will be reviewed. If they decide not to review your Kindle book they'll tell you why. Reviews will be posted on the Book Lovers website, as well as: Amazon, LibraryThing, Goodreads, Facebook and maybe Shelfari.

Goodreads
Link: https://www.goodreads.com/

This website is just a gem. Ideal for readers on the hunt for good books and reviews. Also ideal for new authors who can open a profile and use the numerous free marketing tools offered at the Goodreads author program. At the beginning it is a bit complex to use, but after a while you realise how impressive this readers' and authors' network is. Goodreads is a non-profit organisation.

The readers on the network will click on your book profile if they are planning to read it and afterwards leave their own reviews and comments. Authors can easily interact with their readers and exchange messages.

Book contests could be another good marketing tool to use. Even if you don't win, your book will be listed and your title will be visible.

But why should I pay £100 entry fee without having any guarantee? How do I know the contest is not a scam?

Well, if you are just selling a few books per month, contests might be the perfect pathway to get the push that you need. If you win, your book will be named on specialist websites and also you will have the opportunity to meet many other fellow writers and make great contacts.

I would suggest doing a little research before submitting your book to any contest. Check the details beforehand: look at previous winners, how old the contest is and if your book theme is suited to that specific contest.

Is my writing good enough for contests?
Who does not try does not get.

And what about book cover contests? There are many of them and if you are lucky enough to win one, your book cover will be exposed out there and many people will learn about your book. In those contests no one will put your writing skills under the microscope, but they will look at your creativity and design skills.

Marketing stationery

Another good marketing tool is stationery. Use your books and your company if you have created one as a business tool. I decided to create a brand name with my pseudonym, Maximo Kovak. Everything I do now includes that name and it helps me to create name awareness.

Business cards: I printed business cards using the cover of my first book on one side and my author's name, website, email and details about my social networks accounts on the back. To make full colour business cards today it is not that expensive, about £40 for 500 cards. Every time I see the opportunity, I hand one over, normally to people who are interested in my books or want to know more about me. Around 80% of these people end up buying my book.

Bookmarks: These could be a good idea if you already have in mind some places where you can distribute them, otherwise it will be a waste of money. Also, you will have to get a graphic designer to adapt the design for you to be able to print it out following the printer's requirements.

Posters: Well, you could make some A4 or A3 posters showing the cover of your book, but keep in mind that you will have to find places to put them. I never have done this myself, but some people have had good results by hanging posters in the right places.

Logo and letterheads: Perhaps it wouldn't be a bad idea to get your logo designed and a letterhead sample to use for official documents, and on your website.

There are many other options like pencils, mugs, key holders etc., use your imagination and decide which one will work best for you. Also, think twice before spending money on these things as you need to keep control of your budget.

- What do I really need?
- What stationery can I really afford?
- How will I distribute it?
- Which one could be the most effective for me?

Maximising social networks

Most authors will agree that social networks are a great platform for promotion, but it does not work the same way for everyone and it is not an easy task.

Whether you are a published writer with an agent or an aspiring self-published writer, the challenge is always the same: how to get your name known and how to sell more books. Social networks can be very time consuming and I would say even addictive; however, when used in the right way, they can bring many benefits and help you to promote yourself and your books.

The most popular social networks are Facebook, Twitter, LinkedIn and Google+, but I am sure you know many others.

I am not here to patronise you and tell you how to use social networks, but I will tell you what worked for me and what most people advise when using them.

Whatever is the type of social network that you decide to use, the key question here is how do you attract more people to your profile?

- The main rule is, think about them, not only about you. Generosity and attention attract online friends, arrogance and self-obsession do not.
- Be nice to people and always answer your messages.
- Click "like" or interact when you see something from other users that you like.
- Be honest.
- Be funny, people like a sense of humour.
- Update your profile often and make posts directed to your target audience.
- Be original and find interesting and creative visuals and info that will appeal to the people you are targeting; that way they will share your post or even add you as a friend.

Example 1:
I found a very peculiar photo of a man reading a book, using his feet in a very odd position. I decided to post it on my social networks with a quote saying:

> I always appreciate seeing people who enjoy reading my books
> www.maximokovak.com/books

The post got 400 likes in 3 hours, 30 new people added me on Google+ that day, 10 on Facebook and 5 on Twitter.

Example 2:
I keep my social network profiles on every day so I can check once or twice a day for interesting content. The other day a friend of mine posted a very funny photo where you can see a little notice hanging in a coffee shop window saying: We don't have WiFi. Talk to each other!!

I saved the photo on my computer and I posted it on all my profiles and social groups with a sentence saying: This is my favourite cafe! The response was immediate. Hundreds of likes and comments started to flow during the following hours. Every time someone made a positive comment or clicked "like", I replied or sent them a friend request. I got many new friends that day.

One guy called Peter added me as a friend after he saw my post and started a conversation on Facebook. Apparently my post with the coffee shop notice motivated him to check my profile and then to visit my website link, which was clearly visible on the front. He was the editor of a magazine in the USA and he proposed writing an article about my latest book for his magazine.

You see! Social networks can be time consuming or even superficial sometimes, but you can get many benefits from them if you use them wisely.

A big percentage of my sales come from my social network friends, so I try my best to keep my profiles updated and to get new friend connections.

Your office: being organised

Once you start the process of self-publishing your books you have to be very organised.

First you need a space in your house to file all the documents you will be collecting throughout the process. Receipts, letters, tax documents, invoices, research papers, marketing materials, etc.

Believe me, there will be hundreds of them, so if you are not organised and don't file each one in the right section you will get in trouble later on.

Registering your own business and having a home office has tax advantages. You can declare it as a sole proprietorship and start taking deductions from your income tax.

You should have a clearly defined space in which you carry out all activities related to your business; writing, designing, sending letters and emails, making calls, etc. This could be a spare room or any other space available in your house for such purposes. This space should be used for your business activities and nothing else.

I transformed a small storage space I had in my house into my personal office. I created my working space with a desk, an office chair, filing cabinets, my computer, printer, scanner, file organisers, a lamp and stationery.

Once you have set up your working space you can measure your whole house's square footage and determine how much space is dedicated solely to your business. You can deduct the expenses percentage related to your working space. For example, if your office covers 10% of the total space in your house, you could deduct that same percentage from the rent, mortgage, utility bills, insurance, etc.

You also can deduct the cost of any new equipment or materials you buy to use for your business, a new computer, new filing cabinets, stationery, business cards, book orders, etc. Make sure you keep a record of everything you buy for your office or business.

Many authors also have travel expenses: plane or train tickets, car mileage, and petrol can be also deducted, as long you keep a good record of them.

Having your office space won't promote your book, but it will help you to be very organised and this will positively influence your marketing activity.

Distribute sample chapters

One of the best ways to promote your book is to allow readers to download a table of contents, plus one or more sample chapters from your website. Sample chapters "tease" readers into wanting more. Provided that your sample chapters show competence and an easy reading style, readers will be motivated to buy your book.

Remember that uncertainty is the biggest barrier you must overcome when making a sale to a stranger. In a bookstore, potential buyers can thumb through your book. Online, readers can't do that, so they must depend on sample chapters. Most online self-publishing companies provide the option to give away a sample of your book to potential readers. You can opt to do this when you submit your book to their websites.

Promote your book's URL in your email signature

Give your email recipients a reason to visit your book's website. Don't just list its address, but provide an incentive for them to visit. Arouse their curiosity or offer them a valuable information premium they can download when they visit. This is especially true when you participate in online discussion groups or contribute a comment to an article that invites reader response.

Don't stop promoting one book to start writing another

The buzz and excitement of a book launch can be exhilerating, but the marketing and promotional effort for a book must continue far beyond the early days and weeks of "getting it out there". Include in your marketing plan a schedule that allows for ongoing promotional activities of your previous work, while providing time to write your next book as well.

Rock your book's trailer.

Show your creativity, humour and personality. The advert should be short (less than a minute) and directed at your target audience. Video production is expensive, so do not plan to make a real production with actors and extras, Hollywood style, unless you are 100% sure of what you want to achieve and you have a generous budget.

Self-publishing is about being creative and innovative. You can use the collage video technique where you create a story by pasting together bits of videos and images mixed with music and the messages you want to send. This can be done even without filming anything. Just make a script of the images you need and the message you want to send and get an editor to do it for you. You can get the images from stock video sites or even from Vimeo or YouTube. Using whole videos or parts from someone else's video work is plagiarism; however, if you decide to use extracts from videos already made, you should at least name the artists who made the original in your final video titles and description. This is not necessary when getting stock videos as you've paid for the rights already.

Also, another option for video production (but not necessarily for trailers) could be using Vine. Vine is an app that allows you to make short video loops, and forces you to get to the heart of your message quickly. Fun to make and easy to share, your Vine videos can include a myriad of images and behind-the-scenes glimpses of your writing process, your brand or even your personality.

Free sites for e-book promotion

Some of the web links are very long to add here, but if you Google the main title you will easily find the websites named below.

Addicted to eBooks: This website is perfect for readers who need to watch their book budget. They allow authors to rate some of the content of their book. I want to know before I buy what is the level of profanity, violence or sex in a book. I'm excited that we can now rate our books for the readers.

AppNewser Free eBooks of the Week: The editors pick a few free e-books every week. To submit, email your pitch to appnewser [at] mediabistro [dot] com.

Author Marketing Club: No longer do you have to dig up your links to the best places to submit your books. We've put them all together here for you in one spot. Just click on the logos below to load each site's form, fill in your details, and you're done.

Books on The Knob: Good deal reads, free e-books and book reviews for the Amazon Kindle, nook, Kobo, Sony and other e-readers, Kindle Fire, nookColor, Kobo Vox, and other tablets, with some games, music, technology and computers tossed in now and then.

Digital Book Today: Consists of both free and paid options for writers looking to promote.

eBooks Habit: Every day we will bring you 20-30 great e-books that are free at the time of posting, as well as some bargain e-books with reduced prices!

Ereader News Today: Features Kindle books offers and free Kindle books.

eReader Perks: This site helps people who love to read discover fabulous, new-to-them authors. If you are an author and your book is going to be temporarily free on the Amazon, Kobo, and/or Barnes and Noble websites, use our contact form to get in touch; we will help you spread the word!

Frugal Reader: Use the form to submit your FREE books to be considered for a featured FREEBIE post. Please allow as much time as possible as I know these are limited time offers. Please note that I feature most genres, and while I may feature romance titles that include sexual scenes, I don't feature titles that strictly fall under the erotica genre.

Free Kindle Books & Tips: If you are an author and would like to have your book promoted (for free) on our site, please fill out the form: your book **must** be free in the Amazon Kindle Store and must have an average user rating of at least 4 out of 5 stars for consideration. Please note each book submitted cannot be endorsed due to space limitations.

Free eBooks Daily: I love to hear from authors and readers! If you have a comment or free e-book you would like listed or if you just want to say hello, feel free to send me an email.

GalleyCat Facebook Page: You can post your books in our New Books section, an easy way to share your book with our readers.

Goodkindles: We are a website where you post your own article about your title and can reach readers. We do not review your book – we give you a platform to tell everyone what you think is most attractive about your book and what you think will interest readers so much that they will go and purchase your book.

Meet Our Authors Forum: A place on Amazon where writers can talk about their work.

Pixel of Ink: If your book will be listed as Free ($0.00) on Amazon.com in the next 30 days, then please contact us by filling out our form. Pixel of Ink may attempt to feature your book on the day it is free, time and space permitting.

Blogging

A blog is an essential "hub" for your author marketing efforts. An online presence is now vital for both fiction and non-fiction writers.

Cheaper and easier than a website, a blog can be a one-stop shop for fans and agents to discover your work – or it can make a bad first impression that can never be remedied.

The most significant way to develop a loyal online following is by creating useful content that readers will consume and share. Blogging, at its core, is about offering something of value to your audience.

Here are some additional tips on how to make your blog get real attention:

Determine the purpose of your blog and stick with it. Start by defining for yourself what readers you want to target, and then build a strategy about how to reach them. Be true to the goals you set out for your blog: Are you providing product information? Are you provoking conversation? Are you commenting on trending topics?

Use social media. Make the most of social media by including "Share" on Facebook, Twitter, LinkedIn, Reddit, Google+, and Stumble Upon buttons on your blog. The easier you make it for people to share your content with their network, the more likely they are to do so.

Make sure your content is SEO-friendly. Get smart about search engine optimization. Identify the key words for searching for a posting's subject matter, and think about the best way to incorporate those search terms into the title and body of the post. An invisible blog won't bring you an audience. If you are not good at SEO, then get someone to do it for you. Some people offer basic SEO for reasonable rates. Use the professional finder websites named previously to get an SEO specialist and your blog will get a much bigger audience.

Scheduling your blog. When you're new, set a schedule that you absolutely know you can stick to, no matter what. If that's once a week, start with that. As you get more talented as a blogger, you can always increase the frequency of your posts, and that's usually a good way to increase your traffic and readership.

Here are some of the more popular blog sites:

Blogger is Google's blogging system. Its main benefit is that it's very simple to use and tailor to your needs. It's not as powerful as WordPress; however, unlike WordPress, you can play with the coding and look of your blog in a preview screen. This is a great option for people without a lot of tech knowledge but who have a certain artistic vision of what they want their blog to look like.

A further advantage of Blogger is that you're part of a community of people worldwide.

WordPress is the most sophisticated blogging system available so far. It's an Open Source project, meaning that a worldwide community is frequently helping to develop and upgrade its technology and features.

It also means that it's completely free and substantially expandable. As new plug-ins and technologies are created, these can be added right to your blog. You can either have a free blog hosted at WordPress or you can purchase your own domain, web hosting service, and then download and install WordPress onto the server.

Tumblr and Posterous. The perfect blogging site for people looking for speed and mobility. Some bloggers have gotten tired of having to go through several steps just to post a blog. This has shown the way to new blogging systems set up where you can post just by sending an email. Basically they're just streamlined blogging systems that focus on the content and not any other extra features, which, perhaps involuntarily, leads to a pleasing aesthetic, a kind of minimalist style.

Matador. For some writers, what matters most isn't the structure of a blogging platform, or the features, but simply the opportunity to blog at a place where you're more likely to have a captive audience for your work. Using any of the above platforms, the one disadvantage is that you're just one of millions of other bloggers.

Setting up your blog at a smaller community such as Matador gives surety your writing will gain people's attention.

CONCLUSION

When I started self-publishing books, I was not aware how much hard work was involved in the process; however, I had a great time learning new things about the publishing world.

Over recent years the self-publishing world has boomed and is still growing fast. Many new authors who are rejected by publishers and agents are taking the route of self-publishing. Others even don't bother submitting their book to publishing companies and take the autonomous route from the start.

Publishers and agents don't like taking risks in a publishing market that is already in crisis. So most of them will only take on board reputable and well known authors, or ones who come with a guarantee and are a solid prospect. This leaves new authors like you and me in a dark corner, wondering what to do with our books and passion for writing.

For many years publishers and agents had the power and responsibility to filter book proposals by choosing the writers with most talent and rejecting the uninspiring ones. Their judgement regulated the quality of the books for sale and promoted new, talented authors. Unfortunately the big pressure they are facing today, with a self-publishing market that is taking giant steps, makes their worries grow and they will only publish books with a guaranteed prospect of making a profit.

These fears and their self-interest make them make huge mistakes. For example, there are many cases of new authors who were rejected by publishers and agents who became bestsellers when they self-published their books.

As you can see after reading this guide, there are many things to do to achieve that.

Are you ready?

EMAIL SUPPORT FOR MY READERS

Feel free to contact me if you have any questions related to self-publishing after reading this book.

This service is exclusively available for readers of this book. You will have to supply the **email support code** provided at the end of the book as the headline on your email when you contact me, for me to answer any related questions. Reading the book first will help to avoid unnecessary questions that have been already answered.

CODE: Ayuda1212
EMAIL: contact@maximokovak.com

YOUR REVIEWS AND COMMENTS

If you find this book useful, please leave a review in Amazon or in the website where you bought it.

Your reviews and comments are important for me.

You can follow or contact me through my website or the following social networks:

www.maximokovak.com
Facebook: maximo.kovak
Twitter: @maximokovak
LinkedIn: Maximo kovak
Google+: Maximo Kovak

www.ingramcontent.com/pod-product-compliance
Lightning Source LLC
Chambersburg PA
CBHW071851230426
43671CB00012B/2150